HOW TO WRITE AND CAPTURE YOUR FAMILY YEARBOOK AND STORY

A Story Starter Guide to Write Your Family Stories of the Year

MELANIE JOHNSON AND JENN FOSTER

How to Write and Capture Your Family Yearbook and Story

A Story Starter Guide to Write Your Family Stories of the Year

By Melanie Johnson & Jenn Foster

Write and Capture Your Family Yearbook and Story

2nd Edition
©2016, 2022 Elite Online Publishing

63 East 11400 South
Suite #230
Sandy, UT 84070
EliteOnlinePublishiing.com

ISBN: 978-1-956642-20-9 (eBook)
ISBN: 978-1-956642-18-6 (Paperback)
ISBN: 978-1-956642-19-3 (Hardback)

LAN005060
LAN008000

DEDICATION

To our children! You inspire us every day! We are very proud of your accomplishments and success!

Check out our Free Bonus

Learn how to write your book with our free

guide, 9 Way to Write Your Book Fast

EliteOnlinePublishing.com/9-ways-to-write-a-book-fast

Also visit BestsellersInstitute.com

TABLE OF CONTENTS

ACKNOWLEDGMENTS

Our Kids, Nathan & Justice, for always pushing me and encouraging to do more and be better and keeping me on my toes!! I'm thankful every day that you are my sons.

Bailey, Carson & Brendan, for your patience and support for my business. You help me understand the meaning of life! I feel so blessed to have you all in my life.

Our Families, for all the support, love and standing by us through thick and thin.

Mike Koenigs, thank you for inspiring us to become authors and start our publishing business.

Chris & Pam Hendrickson, thanks for all your motivational videos and products. We love seeing you speak on stage!

Paul Colligan, thank you for inspiring and encouraging us to be brave enough to start our own podcast.

Darren Hardy, thank you for your daily inspirational emails. You push us to do better and better each day.

Tony Robbins, thank you for giving us strategies to make life easier.

And everyone else we may have forgotten to give thanks and praise to. We Thank you Very Much!

INTRODUCTION

If you have wanted to write and keep a journal of your family's journey of the year, you have come to the right place. You will be so happy that you have chosen to write in this journal that will leave a legacy for generations to come.

You will be leaving a slice of history by sharing you and your family's personal journey. The *Family Story Starter* will turn your stories and memories into a treasured book for years to come. The book is designed to be filled out either every month or one time per year, quarter, or season. It's impactful when everyone in the family has their own book and you do it together, sharing it along the way.

It's a great idea to have each family member receive their own book, then you can compare each other's stories. We assure you'll laugh at the different stories everyone has.

By answering the questions in this book, you will see how easy and fun it is to record all the special moments, memories and events of your family.

Most importantly you will be creating a legacy for your family, grandchildren, and great grandchildren.

Check out Melanie Johnson's TEDx Talk on YouTube. Search "Leaving a Legacy - The Time is Now" (https://youtu.be/aXyLNrnl7OE)

This book is designed to capture a piece of who you and your family members are right now and create memories you can celebrate for the rest of your life.

THE BEST TIME TO WRITE

The Family Story Starter can be started on any day of the year.

It works great to have a time of day to write in your *Family Story Starter*. You may like to write first thing in the morning or at night, before you fall asleep. Choose a time that works best for you. You can do it yourself or one or more of your family members can do it with you.

It's okay if you skip a day or two. Feel free to jot down notes to remind you throughout the day of what you want to write about, you can always come back to it later. That's the beauty of keeping a journal, you can write however or whenever you'd like.

WAYS TO ENJOY YOUR BOOK

Sharing is caring. The best way to totally enjoy this journal is to share it with others. You can read the stories out loud at bedtime, to create special family nights.

Families everywhere are discovering that reading-aloud is one of the most powerful ways to connect with your kids and keep your family strong.

MAKE IT A GAME

This is a great way for the whole family to have fun and create memories at the same time. Each family member will have their own copy of the *Family Story Starter*.

Each person will have written their answers down. Take one of the questions from the book and other family members can try to guess the answers to one of the OTHER family members.

For example: What do you think one of the children wrote down as their top Goals. What was brother's favorite restaurant, how would they describe a typical day and you could do this acting in the character of the person.

The person with the most correct

answers wins the game. You will laugh and learn more about your kids in a fun way. A beautiful way to create family memories. It will be a game you can look forward to playing with them every month or season.

This is great to play during a road trip to help pass the time.

3 Ways to Write In Your Journal Without Actually Writing In It.

1. Don't write in your journal longhand. Talk the answers of your journal instead. You can use the app "Evernote" or "Otter.ai" to talk your story and the app will transcribe it as you go. Otter gives you an audio recording as well as the transcript.
2. You can talk into your phone on "Notes" and it will transcribe it for you.
3. You can video yourself using your phone and a selfie stick and have it transcribed.
4. You can listen to the book using the

Alexa or using the Alexa app on your phone. The app is great to use in the car. Imagine using it going to and from school each day. Asking the questions, engaging in conversation with your kids vs them just sitting on their iPad. You can even run the otter app or note transcription in the background and record their answers.

TIPS:

- When using Evernote or Notes, you may have to talk slower and more precise, so it will keep up with you. We all tend to talk really fast, so you may have to slow down.
- The cool thing about video is that you can save it for later and upload it to YouTube. You can share it privately to just family and friends or you can share it to the whole world.
- Here are some websites we recommend finding a transcriber:

Upwork.com

33

fiverr.com

QUESTION AND ANSWER

This book is full of questions to get you thinking about the stories in your family's life. To open your mind about your life, goals and achievements. But before you dive in and answer the questions, it's time to get your mindset ready and your brain turned on!

Now it's time to jump in and start your story. In the following chapters you will uncover answers to some of the best moments and memories your days and months You will laugh and cry as you write or tell the stories that are special to you. It may trigger emotions you haven't felt in a long time, recalling a person you haven't thought of in years. Take the opportunity to reach out to them and remember old times and renew your friendship. This book is about you and your family's story but it's so much more than that. It's capturing your legacy and taking you through time. It would be great to sit around the family room with your children and grandchildren answering the questions. You may even consider doing the book as a fun party with your siblings or best friends all answering the questions together. Think about maybe recording it on otter.ai or zoom.

Tips:

- Feel free to do it in any order that feels the most comfortable for you. If you are like me, you may jump around answering questions from different chapters during the same session.

- Don't feel overwhelmed that you must finish the book all at one sitting. A couple great strategies are to answer a couple questions each morning to start your day or at the end of the day before you go to bed.

- When answering the questions think of Why you did it, When and how did you do it, Specific ways it has changed your life. Give as much detail as you can remember. So, the reader can feel like they were there. For example, what was the weather like that day, what were your surroundings, the smell in the air, what did you wear. Etc.

- Be vulnerable. When you let yourself be vulnerable and transparent, something magical happens. "Vulnerability is a powerful thing in storytelling because it creates a human connection unlike anything else." You will not just be answering questions, but creating a very personal and memorable connection with your reader.

- Most of all have fun! Laugh, cry, ponder and reflect. Enjoy the journey whether you write it cozied up in your favorite chair or with a bunch of your family and friends.

GET YOUR HEAD IN THE GAME

BE OPEN - Allow yourself to be open to getting out of your comfort zone. Be Vulnerable. Here is a great TED talk on being vulnerable by Brene Brown.

https://youtu.be/iCvmsMzlF7o

KNOW YOUR WHY- You must know the reason why you are writing in your Family Story Starter. What is your purpose? What do you want the outcome to be? How do you want your family/friends/readers to feel after they read your journal? What lessons, benefits or insights will they gain?

VISUALIZE- Picture how you will feel once you have finished your journal and ready to start your next one. Imagine what it's like to have completed sharing the journal with your family and friends.

PLACES- Pick a special place to write or record your book. It can be a place that is special to you or that is quiet, where you can focus.

NEVER GIVE UP- If for some reason you miss a day, a week or even a month or you are still sitting with this journal on your desk and you haven't even started, don't beat yourself up, just try again. Today is a new day and the perfect day to get started.

MINDSET MAKEOVER

HAPPY DAYS ARE HERE AGAIN!

Here are some great ways to get in a positive mindset while you are writing in your Family Story Starter. Practice all or some of these. Not only will they put you in a great mood to write in your journal, they will improve your everyday life. Happiness is a choice, choose it every day!

Gratitude- When you feel there should be more

to life, take an inventory of what you already have. Your health, family, friends, a place to live, clothes to wear, food to eat, your skills and your dreams.

Giving- This makes us happier and healthier and it creates stronger connections between people. You can give your time, your ideas and your smile.

Exercising- Take care of your body; it's the only one you've got. The body and mind are connected. Being active makes us happier, improves our mood, helps us sleep better and gives us a strong energetic body.

Live in the Moment- Appreciate the world around you, even noticing the breeze rustling the leaves on a tree.

Grow- Keep learning new things. It gives us a sense of accomplishment and improves our wellbeing. It helps us stay curious and engaged.

Have Goals- This gives us something to look forward to. Feeling good about our future is important for happiness. Goals excite us and motivate us. They give us direction.

Emotion- Research shows that regularly experiencing joy, gratitude, contentment, inspiration, and pride creates an upward momentum in our spirit.

Acceptance- Love who you are. Be kind to yourself. Don't dwell on who you are not or compare yourself to others. We each have our unique gifts and talents and we should celebrate each other.

Purpose and Meaning- Be a part of something bigger. Leave a legacy and tell your story. People who have meaning and purpose in their lives are happier and live longer.

Motivation- Find your "Why". It could be a goal, something you love, something you hate, or something you are passionate about.

Journaling- This releases the thoughts from the day or week. This helps us reflect and release everything that is rattling around in our head and put it down on paper.

Gratitude Journal- Write down the 5-10 things you are grateful for each day. Oprah says doing this one thing will change your life.

Read or Listen to Something Inspiring- Fill your head with positive, healthy, energizing, thoughts. This is health food for the brain.

Meditate or Pray- Take some quiet time for your mind to be at peace and rest with your creator.

Do an Activity as a Family- This will bond you together and create a memory.

Perform Random Acts of Kindness- If you want something you should give it away and then it will come back to you. If you want love, give love; if you want a mentor, be a mentor.

Create a Vision Board- Fill this with pictures of goals you would like to achieve and experience. Examples are: vacations, cars, houses, and romance.

Wake Up to Happy Music- Why not start your day on a upbeat, happy note! Pick music that has meaning to you and puts a smile on your face.

Dance Like Nobody's Watching- Really, turn on some music and go full-tilt crazy dancing. Watch how your mood will change.

Sweet Dreams- Think of a few things that really make you happy, or something you would like to experience that would put a smile on your face before you go to bed. You are programming your mind for what you want to dream about. People wake up happier when they have had a happy or positive dream the night before.

Breathe- Your body is primarily made up of water. It is 70% water and thrives on oxygen. Most of us don't breathe enough, especially if we don't do a great cardio workout. When we are stressed we tend to breathe shallowly. If you are like me, you hold your breath when stressing about things. Here is a quick tip. Take 10 deep breaths in for 4 seconds, holding each one for 4 seconds, then breath out for 6 seconds. Do this 3 times a day. Do it in the morning, in your car, while you are walking the dog, and lying in bed before you go to sleep. You will have more energy and be more relaxed and your mind will think more clearly.

Eat Well- Water, water, water! 70% of your diet should contain water rich foods. That means fruits and vegetables. Try this exercise; write down what you ate for the last 24 hours and see how much of it came from the earth versus pre-packaged.

You Are the Company You Keep- Stay away from the character Eeyore from Winnie the Pooh. Even though you're happy an energized attitude will be contiguous. People that live in the black abyss can suck you in. Limit your time from the terminal Eeyore types. Take inventory of the company you keep. Research shows you will start to take on the traits of the company you regularly keep. If they are always eating ice cream, before you know it, you will be eating ice cream with them. If they always use certain words or phrases, you will find that you start using some of the same words and phrases. (Just saying!)

Give a Compliment- It's amazing how someone's face will light up when you give them a sincere compliment. What happens afterward is that you get a warm fuzzy feeling inside knowing you have brightened someone's day.

Sleep Your Way to the Top- Getting enough sleep is imperative. Your brain doesn't function at full speed when you are sleep deprived. There is nothing pretty about being burnt out and exhausted.

Eat an Apple a Day- The saying is NOT eat a cookie a day. Think of the small stuff and the compound effect over time it will have. What if you did replace that cookie or cupcake with an apple or a piece of fruit? What would the result be after one week, one month, one year? It's the small things that will make a major difference in your life.

Smile, DAMN IT! - The best way to immediately reduce stress is to SMILE. Your body naturally relaxes when you smile. Wake up and smile before your feet hit the ground. When you first look into the mirror in the morning smile at yourself. Guess what? You'll be smiling right back at yourself. Isn't it nice to wake up to a happy face?

"Smile - It Increases Your Face Value!"
- Dolly Parton

Give Yourself a Hug- Literally wrap your arms around yourself and squeeze for a whole minute or so, take a few deep breaths and smile.

Own Happiness, Health and Productivity- Act Happy, talk like you're happy, walk like you're happy, think like you're happy, smile like you're happy, dress like you're happy. Put the actions behind your intention and they will become a reality.

P.S. I Love YOU!- First off, give yourself love. It's not enough to say it in your head. Stand in front of a mirror, look at yourself for about one minute or so in silence, gazing at all that you are and then say, "I Love you, I really love you." This practice has brought some people to tears the first time they do it. Now think of the people you love in your life and mentally send love to them. Then visualize how they will respond and look at you when they feel you love them. Now that's a pretty picture!

"We all have a life story and a message that can inspire others to live a better life or run a better business. Why not use that story and message to serve others"

-Brendon Burchard

THE LIFE OF OUR FAMILY

"It is a wise and loving gift to write one's story. It is a family treasure made of words."

1. Describe what a typical day looks like in your family. This could be for the week, the month, or season. For example, the first week of school is starting. You or the kids are starting a new project. You are getting ready for the holidays or vacation etc.

_____

_____

_____

_____

_____

_____

_____

_____

_____

_____

_____

_____

_____

2. Who are you hanging out with?

_____

_____

_____

_____

_____

_____

_____

_____

_____

_____

_____

_____

_____

_____

3. Where is everyone living? This can include grandparents and other close family members.

_____

_____

_____

_____

_____

_____

_____

_____

_____

_____

_____

_____

_____

_____

4. Who works, attends school, etc.? Where?

_____

_____

_____

_____

_____

_____

_____

_____

_____

_____

_____

_____

_____

_____

_____

_____

5. What responsibilities does each family member have in the family and home?

_____

_____

_____

_____

_____

_____

_____

_____

_____

_____

_____

_____

_____

6. What are some favorite pastimes your family is currently enjoying?

_____

_____

_____

_____

_____

_____

_____

_____

_____

_____

_____

_____

_____

_____

_____

_____

7. After school/work what does each family member do?

_____

_____

_____

_____

_____

_____

_____

_____

_____

_____

_____

_____

_____

_____

_____

8. Describe the home and any changes that took place over this month.

_____

_____

_____

_____

_____

_____

_____

_____

_____

_____

_____

_____

_____

_____

_____

9. What were some of the major world or local headlines of the year and how did they impact your family?

_____

_____

_____

_____

_____

_____

_____

_____

_____

_____

_____

_____

_____

_____

10. What are each of your family member's favorite dinners. What do you like to cook, order out or restaurants you like to visit?

_____

_____

_____

_____

_____

_____

_____

_____

_____

_____

_____

_____

_____

_____

11. Describe what your are grateful for.

_____

_____

_____

_____

_____

_____

_____

_____

_____

_____

_____

_____

_____

_____

12. What are each of your family member's favorite desserts or ice cream flavors? What are the favorites to make at home and where do you usually go for ice cream or dessert?

_____

_____

_____

_____

_____

_____

_____

_____

_____

_____

_____

_____

_____

_____

Melanie Johnson & Jenn Foster

MONTHLY ACTIVITIES

"You are history, and history disappears if you don't record it."

- Frank P. Thomas

Review each month of the year. Create a photo collage or choose a photo for each month and answer the following questions.

1. What holidays took place this month?

_____

_____

_____

_____

_____

_____

_____

_____

_____

_____

_____

_____

_____

_____

_____

_____

2. How did you celebrate the holidays?

_____

_____

_____

_____

_____

_____

_____

_____

_____

_____

_____

_____

_____

_____

_____

3. Who celebrated the holidays with you?

_____

_____

_____

_____

_____

_____

_____

_____

_____

_____

_____

_____

_____

_____

_____

_____

4. Did anyone celebrate a birthday this month? How old is that person?

_____

_____

_____

_____

_____

_____

_____

_____

_____

_____

_____

_____

_____

5. How was the birthday celebrated?

_____

_____

_____

_____

_____

_____

_____

_____

_____

_____

_____

_____

_____

_____

_____

6. What other significant events took place this month?

_____

_____

_____

_____

_____

_____

_____

_____

_____

_____

_____

_____

_____

_____

7. Did any of your celebration include family traditions?

_____

_____

_____

_____

_____

_____

_____

_____

_____

_____

_____

_____

_____

_____

8. This month, did a family member accomplish or achieve something?

_____

_____

_____

_____

_____

_____

_____

_____

_____

_____

_____

_____

_____

_____

_____

9. Were there difficult situations that the family faced?

_____

_____

_____

_____

_____

_____

_____

_____

_____

_____

_____

_____

_____

_____

10. If so, how were those situates dealt with?

_____

_____

_____

_____

_____

_____

_____

_____

_____

_____

_____

_____

_____

_____

_____

READ ALL ABOUT IT

"Storytelling is the most powerful way to put ideas into the world today."

- Robert McAffee Brown

1. How old are your family members?

_____

_____

_____

_____

_____

_____

_____

_____

_____

_____

_____

_____

_____

_____

2. What activities does each person participate in during the year? (Sports, community service, lessons, trips, etc.)

_____

_____

_____

_____

_____

_____

_____

_____

_____

_____

_____

_____

_____

_____

3. Who played a special role in each family member's life during the year? (Friends, mentors, employers, teachers, etc.)

_____

_____

_____

_____

_____

_____

_____

_____

_____

_____

_____

_____

_____

_____

4. What was a typical day/week in each person's life during this month or season?

_____

_____

_____

_____

_____

_____

_____

_____

_____

_____

_____

_____

_____

_____

_____

5. What special accomplishments did each of you achieve?

_____

_____

_____

_____

_____

_____

_____

_____

_____

_____

_____

_____

_____

_____

6. Were there any disappointments? How did he/she overcome them?

_____

_____

_____

_____

_____

_____

_____

_____

_____

_____

_____

_____

_____

_____

_____

7. Describe some of each person's fears, dreams, and aspirations.

_____

_____

_____

_____

_____

_____

_____

_____

_____

_____

_____

_____

_____

8. What were each person's favorite hobbies, books, music, movies, television shows, games, etc.?

_____

_____

_____

_____

_____

_____

_____

_____

_____

_____

_____

_____

_____

9. What does each person's bedroom look like?

_____

_____

_____

_____

_____

_____

_____

_____

_____

_____

_____

_____

_____

_____

10. What trips did each person go on during the month?

_____

_____

_____

_____

_____

_____

_____

_____

_____

_____

_____

_____

_____

_____

OUR MONTH

"Write it on your heart that every day is the best day in the year."

-Ralph Waldo Emerson

1. This month I learned to...

_____

_____

_____

_____

_____

_____

_____

_____

_____

_____

_____

_____

_____

_____

2. Right now I'm obsessed with...

_____

_____

_____

_____

_____

_____

_____

_____

_____

_____

_____

_____

_____

_____

_____

_____

3. Service: How did the family serve the community?

_____

_____

_____

_____

_____

_____

_____

_____

_____

_____

_____

_____

_____

_____

4. Friends and extended family (Who married, graduated, etc.?)

_____

_____

_____

_____

_____

_____

_____

_____

_____

_____

_____

_____

_____

_____

_____

5. Headlines: How current events impacted us.

_____

_____

_____

_____

_____

_____

_____

_____

_____

_____

_____

_____

_____

_____

_____

_____

6. On the weekends I liked to...

_____

_____

_____

_____

_____

_____

_____

_____

_____

_____

_____

_____

_____

_____

_____

_____

7. Our favorites (recreation, restaurants, pastimes, music, etc.)

_____

_____

_____

_____

_____

_____

_____

_____

_____

_____

_____

_____

_____

_____

8. Milestones we met and triumphs we celebrated.

_____

_____

_____

_____

_____

_____

_____

_____

_____

_____

_____

_____

_____

_____

_____

_____

9. How our family numbers changed (births & deaths).

_____

_____

_____

_____

_____

_____

_____

_____

_____

_____

_____

_____

_____

_____

10. What challenges have you overcome?

_____

_____

_____

_____

_____

_____

_____

_____

_____

_____

_____

_____

_____

_____

_____

_____

11. Where do you want to be one year from now? Goals and Dreams.

_____

_____

_____

_____

_____

_____

_____

_____

_____

_____

_____

_____

_____

_____

12. Where do you want to be three years from now? Goals and Dreams.

_____

_____

_____

_____

_____

_____

_____

_____

_____

_____

_____

_____

_____

_____

_____

13. How have your grown this month? What has changed you or members of your family?

_____

_____

_____

_____

_____

_____

_____

_____

_____

_____

_____

_____

_____

_____

POP CULTURE

"One thing I've learned is that I'm not the owner of my talent; I'm the manager of it."

–Madonna Ciccone

1. Major headlines of the year.

_____

_____

_____

_____

_____

_____

_____

_____

_____

_____

_____

_____

_____

_____

_____

2. What things were major discussions at school, work, neighborhood, etc.

_____

_____

_____

_____

_____

_____

_____

_____

_____

_____

_____

_____

_____

_____

3. What were some of the fashion trends? (Hair, clothes, accessories, etc.)

_____

_____

_____

_____

_____

_____

_____

_____

_____

_____

_____

_____

_____

_____

4. What was the price of gas, milk, bread, movie tickets, pizza, etc.?

_____

_____

_____

_____

_____

_____

_____

_____

_____

_____

_____

_____

_____

5. What were your favorite movies, music, TikTok, Reels & T.V. shows?

_____

_____

_____

_____

_____

_____

_____

_____

_____

_____

_____

_____

_____

_____

6. Who were important political figures and/or scandals?

_____

_____

_____

_____

_____

_____

_____

_____

_____

_____

_____

_____

_____

_____

_____

_____

7. Who were some of your favorite popular entertainers?

_____

_____

_____

_____

_____

_____

_____

_____

_____

_____

_____

_____

_____

_____

_____

8. What were popular fashion, decorating colors, or trends?

_____

_____

_____

_____

_____

_____

_____

_____

_____

_____

_____

_____

_____

_____

_____

9. What were some of the popular phrases and lingo?

_____

_____

_____

_____

_____

_____

_____

_____

_____

_____

_____

_____

_____

_____

10. What were some of your favorite places to shop and/or "hang out"?

_____

_____

_____

_____

_____

_____

_____

_____

_____

_____

_____

_____

_____

_____

11. What were the bestselling books? Did you read them? Give your review?

_____

_____

_____

_____

_____

_____

_____

_____

_____

_____

_____

_____

_____

_____

_____

12. What is the latest "hot" technology? How have you used it?

_____

_____

_____

_____

_____

_____

_____

_____

_____

_____

_____

_____

_____

_____

_____

13. Describe local traditions and community events. Did You participate?

_____

_____

_____

_____

_____

_____

_____

_____

_____

_____

_____

_____

_____

_____

What's Next

Congratulations! If you are on this page that means you have finished your questions and your family legacy has begun. Way to go!

If you are ever inclined to publish your work we can help you do just that.

An author we worked with at first just wanted to print 20 copies for his family, then when the world got out, friends and family from all over the country wanted a copy. We ended up putting it for sale on Amazon and it sells copies every month. The other choice is to print copies at a local printer and mail them out yourself to all those clamoring to get a copy.

Before you can print the book, there still is a little bit of work to do. You'll want to have a beautiful book cover design. We use a team of graphic artists for our clients, but you can find book cover designers on Fiverr.com or Upwork. You can hire a book formatter there too. Formatting is taking your word document and turning it into a professional ready for print, PDF document.

Before you send it to the formatter have it looked over by either a professional editor or have someone you trust edit it.

Now it's time to publish your book. You may be saying I don't have the slightest idea to do that. We are here to help. We have a digital video training course for publishing, or you can hire us one on one.

Visit BestsellerSolutions.com

"I think I did pretty well, considering I started out with nothing but a bunch of blank paper."

– Steve Martin

ABOUT THE AUTHORS

Melanie Churella Johnson

Melanie is a WSJ/USA Today bestselling author and 16x Amazon bestseller. She launched, owned, and operated a $100 million media company with TV stations in Houston and Dallas Texas: Houston (Channel 51) and Dallas (Channel 55). Melanie started her career as a News Anchor in Detroit at Channel 20 after she won the title of Miss

Michigan and was first runner up to Miss America. Melanie has a background in Media, Marketing, Public Relations and Advertising. She has been in front of, as well as behind the camera. She was a News Anchor, Producer, Writer, Public Relations, Promotions, TV ad sales, Programming negotiations and Financial Strategist. She has done business with Warner Brothers, Disney, King World and MGM Studios. In addition to creating and developing successful businesses she has created award winner advertising campaigns.

Melanie is the CEO and co-owner of Elite Online Publishing. They publish, market, and promote nonfiction books for business owners and athletes to create expert authority status for marketing impact and influence. She is passionate about sharing people's stories that educate, motivate, and inspire. She is honored to work one on one with their authors to create the best strategies for their book creation, marketing, and social media.

Melanie was honored to be a TEDx speaker in Sugarland, Texas in 2016, where she spoke on the importance of leaving a legacy. She is the co-host of the Elite Expert Insider podcast on iTunes and Stitcher Radio and has a YouTube channel.

She got her feet wet in the luxury building and design industry when she was the general contractor and developer for her personal 25,000 square foot home known as "The

Houston Mansion" and her 13,000 square foot summer home in Petoskey, Michigan "The Walloon Lake House." During the economic downturn, Melanie turned both of these properties into successful Luxury Vacation and Event Rental Properties and continues to invest and develop real estate.

She is the CEO of Charity Auction Consignments. Melanie graciously donates her Villa in the Dominican Republic along with her other properties to help raise money for children's issues, health, education, and animals. She works with numerous charities including Texas Children's Hospital, Citizens for Animal Protection, Fanatical Change Foundation, Just Like My Child Foundation and a variety of private schools.

Melanie graduated from Michigan State University with a degree in communications and was the first girl to receive a varsity letter in a boys sport in the state of Michigan. She lives in Houston, Texas and is originally from Michigan. She is enjoying raising her two sons, who keep her motivated and young. She loves the beach, traveling and spending time with her family.

Follow Melanie at:

AuthorMelanieJohnson.com

Facebook.com/authormelaniejohnson

Instagram.com/melaniecjohnson

LinkedIn.com/in/melaniejohnson-eop

Eliteonlinepublishing.com

JENN FOSTER

Jenn is a Wall Street Journal, USA Today and International bestselling author. She is the owner of Elite Online Publishing and Biz Social Marketing Agency. Companies dedicated to helping business owners of all sizes thrive in today's highly technical world of product and service promotion. Jenn owned and operated a successful local chain of retail stores, where she honed her online marketing skills. From local brick and mortar stores to online entities, to large international corporations, Jenn's years of experience and expertise have now helped hundreds of businesses become front page news on major search engines. She is dedicated to helping businesses use powerful new online and mobile marketing platforms to get visibility, traffic, leads, customers, and raving fans. She is passionate about helping busy entrepreneurs, business leaders, and professionals to create, publish, and market their book, to build their business and brand. She encourages new authors to share their stories, knowledge, and expertise to help others. With her marketing and digital background, Jenn uses the best strategies for her client's books to boost their sales and marketing platforms and helps them achieve #1 bestselling status.

A graduate of Utah State University, Jenn is an award-winning web designer, author and sought after speaker. She has been a featured panelist and speaker at events with experts like Loral Langemier, Lisa Sasevich, Mike Koenigs, Ed Rush and more. Jenn has been named one of America's Premier Experts® and is highlighted in the Dan Kennedy Book, *Stand Apart*. Jenn Foster was recently named one of "Utah's Thought Leaders" in the book *Innovate Utah* by Global Village. Jenn is the co-host of Elite Expert Insider Podcast on iTunes and Spotify.

Coming from a family of successful entrepreneurs, her grandfather started the Maverik Country Stores oil and gas station chain which is still thriving today. Jenn grew up around successful businesses and understands from the ground up what it takes to create, run and promote winning companies. Combining her education, knowledge, and life-long experience, today Jenn teaches people and businesses globally how they can get found in today's virtual world, how they can engage prospects on their terms and how to continue to connect and follow up with prospects to convert them to customers.

Jenn is a single Mom who loves spending time with her three children, traveling, and experiencing the great outdoors.

Follow Jenn Foster:

AuthorJennFoster.com

Eliteonlinepublishing.com

Facebook.com/authorjennfoster

Instagram.com/jennfosterchic

LinkedIn.com/in/jennfosterseo

ELITE
ONLINE
PUBLISHING

About Elite Online Publishing

We believe you have a story to tell, and we know that the lives of your readers will be vastly improved from learning from your expertise.

That's why we help authors write, market, and publish a book they can be proud of. With our full-service publishing packages, we help you build your book from start to finish, develop your personal brand that speaks to your expertise, then create an insatiable buzz that launches you to Bestseller status.

Our greatest pride comes from our ability to turn ordinary business leaders with little to no writing experience into accomplished authors who top the charts and become instant authorities. Many of our authors have beat out books published by authors like Tina Fey, Tim Ferris, and Robin Williams. We help authors find their voice through writing workshops, masterclasses, and content creation of digital courses. Our collaborations last long past launch day, all our authors are part of the Elite Online Publishing family.

Whether you want to publish an eBook, paperback, hardback, or audiobook we'll ensure your book reaches the top of the bestseller list. *Elite Online Publishing's services* also include video production, Amazon author page design, social media posting, website design, and management to ensure your success grows. With us, you'll get individualized assistance and hands-on support to craft the story you were meant to share.

When we're not publishing chart-topping books, founders and owners Melanie Johnson & Jenn Foster interview inspirational speakers and entrepreneurs on Elite Publishing's podcast, *Elite Expert Insider*. And *Elite Publishing Podcast*.

To get your book published visit

EliteOnlinePublishing.com

Subscribe to our Podcast on iTunes or anywhere you listen to podcasts - Look for Elite Expert Insider. **Elite.libsyn.com**

Subscribe to our YouTube Channel

YouTube.com/eliteonlinepublishing1

Check out our Free Bonus

Learn how to write your book with our free

guide, 9 Way to Write Your Book Fast

EliteOnlinePublishing.com/9-ways-to-write-a-book-fast

Also visit BestsellerSolutions.com